Antique Fruit Prints
- An Adult Coloring Book -

Want to see the original antique prints to colorize your own artwork?

Visit our website at www.BotanicalArtDesigns.com. Click on the book cover image in the Book Images section and view the original colored images in PDF format.

ISBN-10: 1533272204
ISBN-13: 978-1533272201

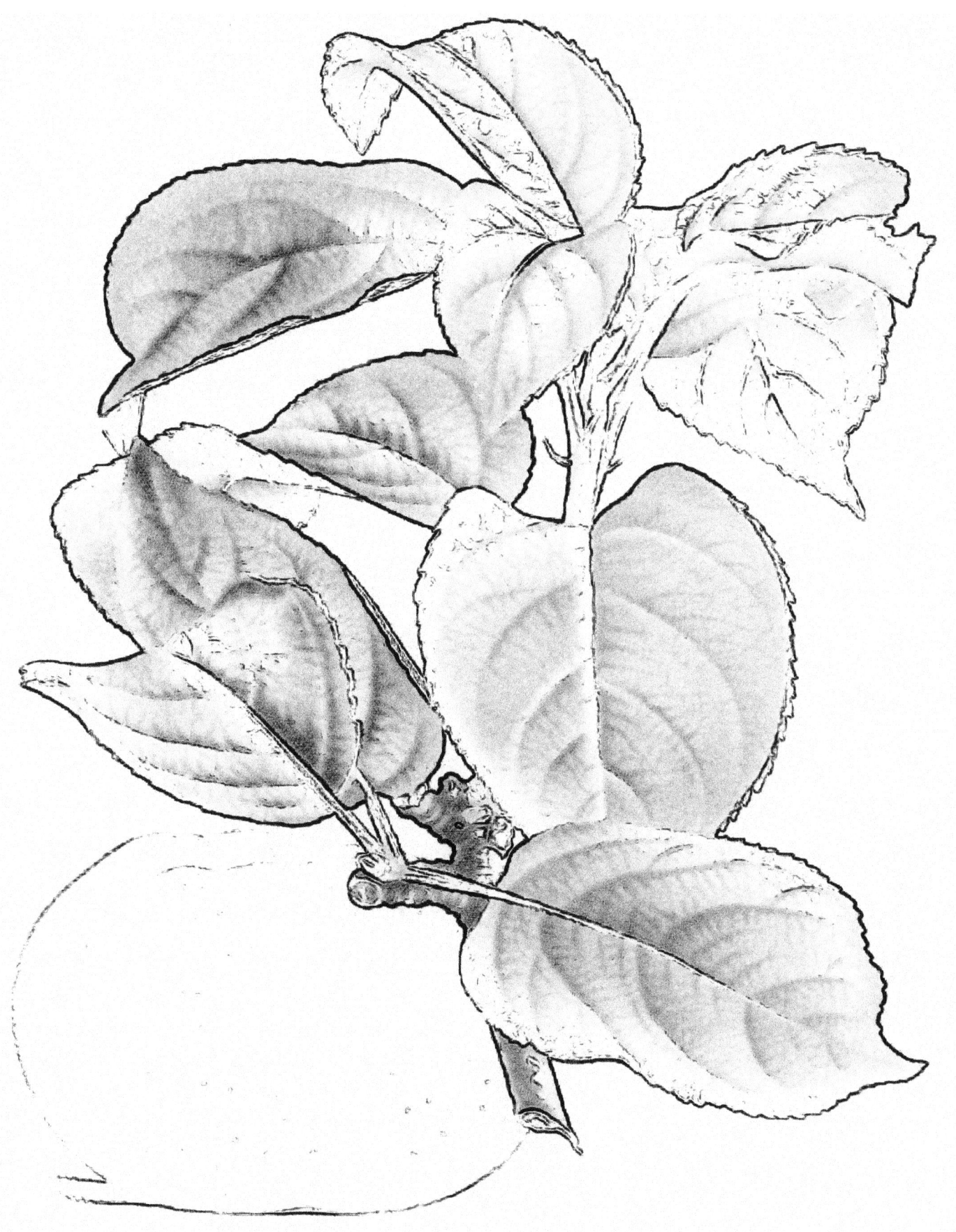

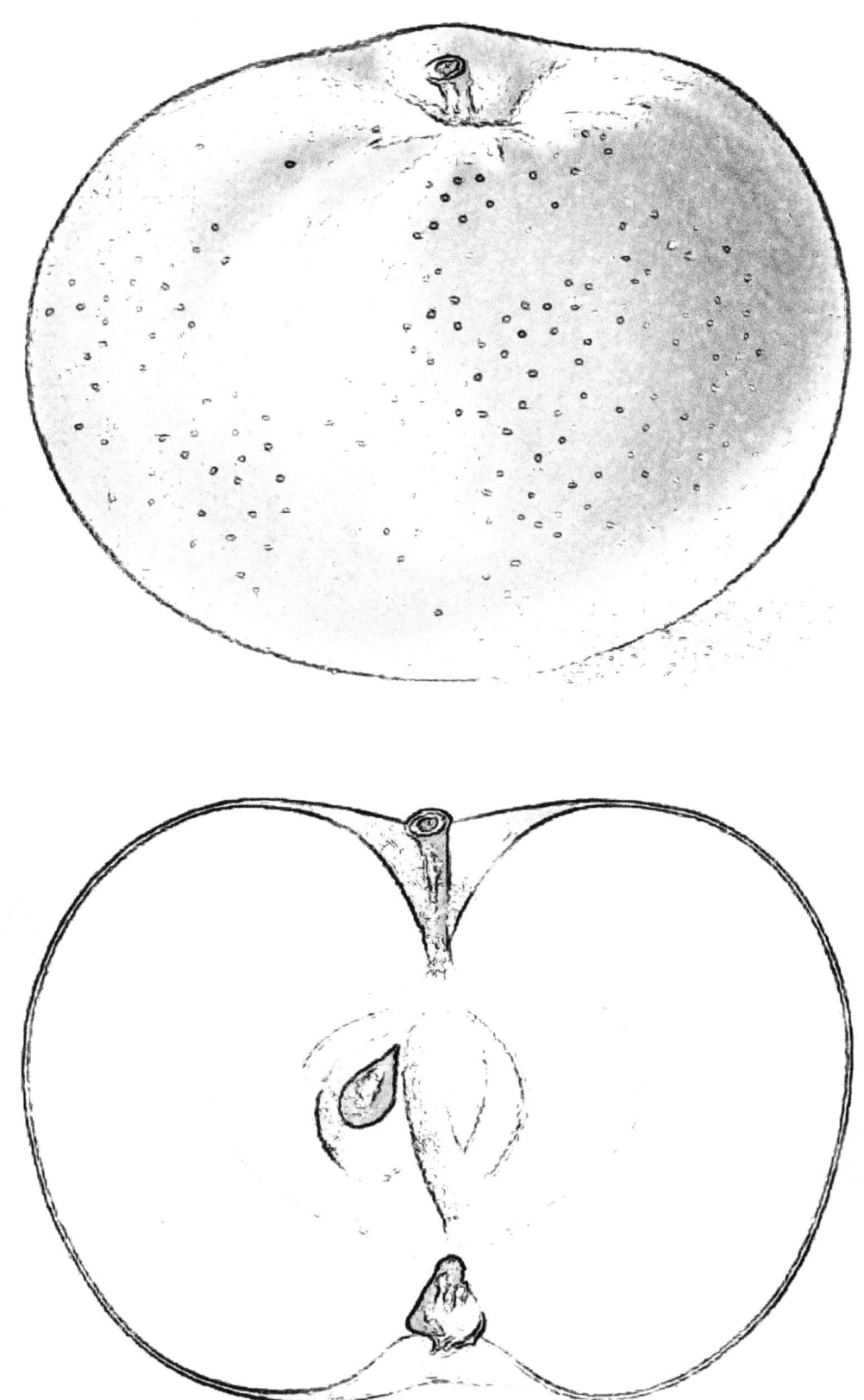

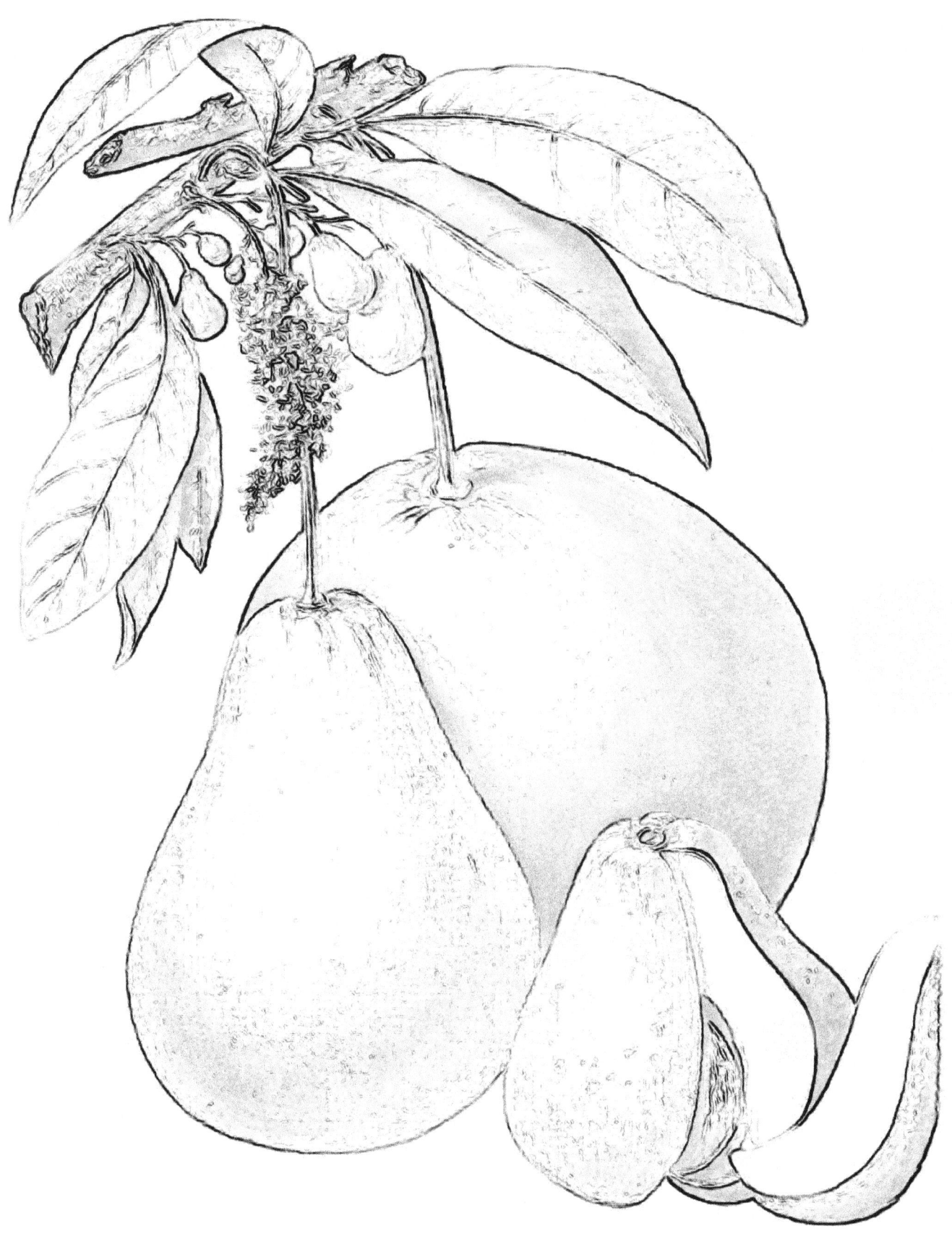

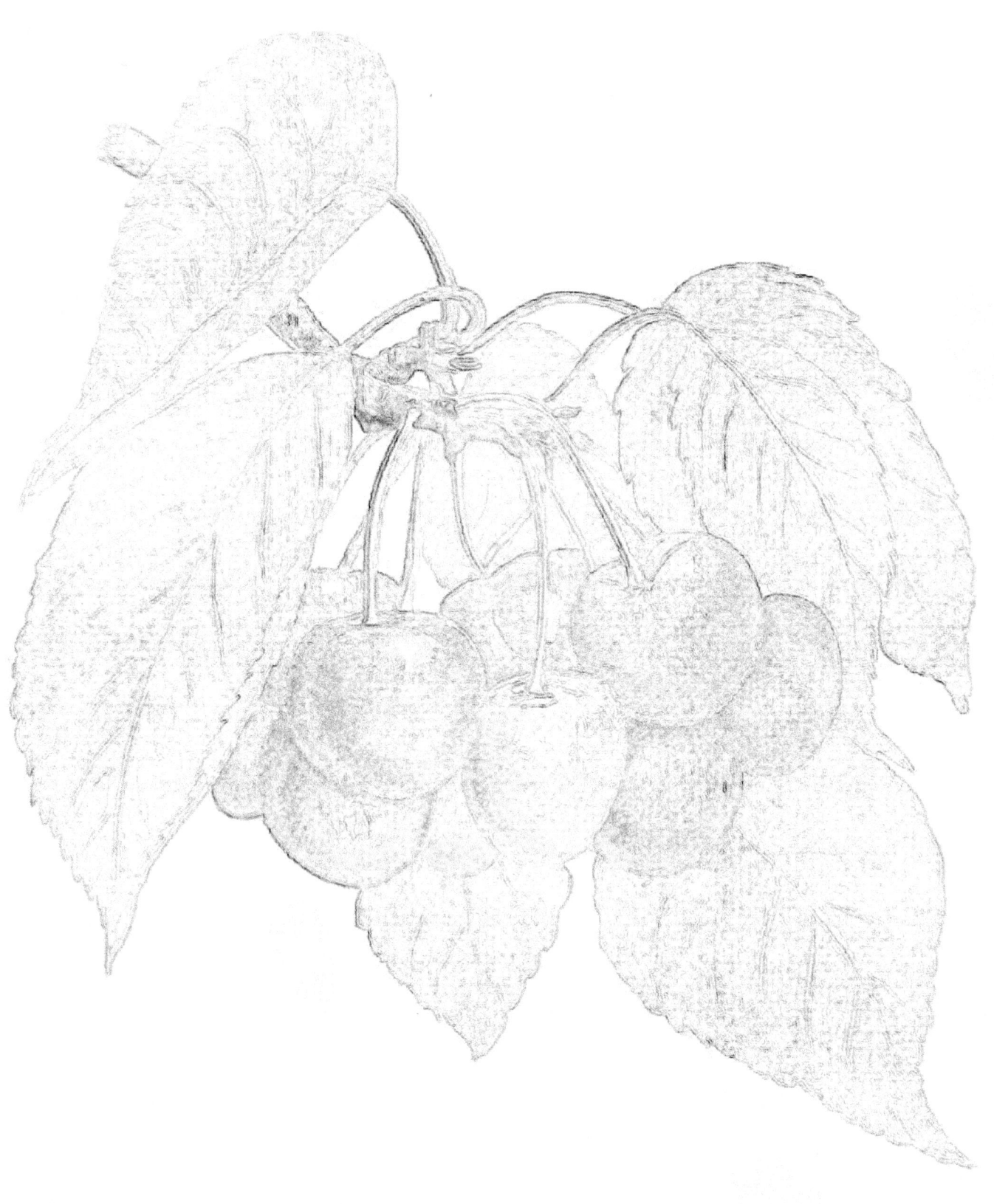

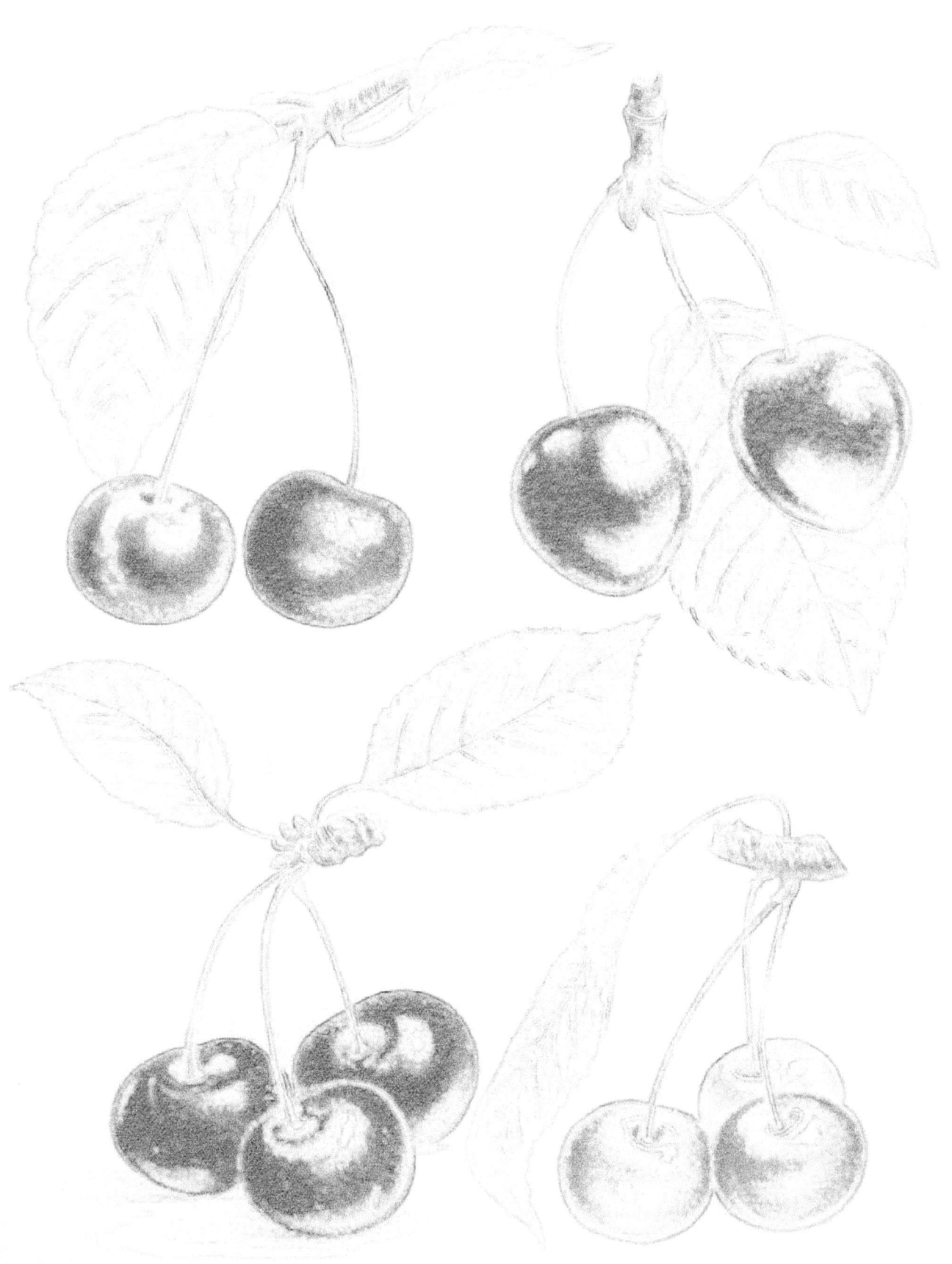

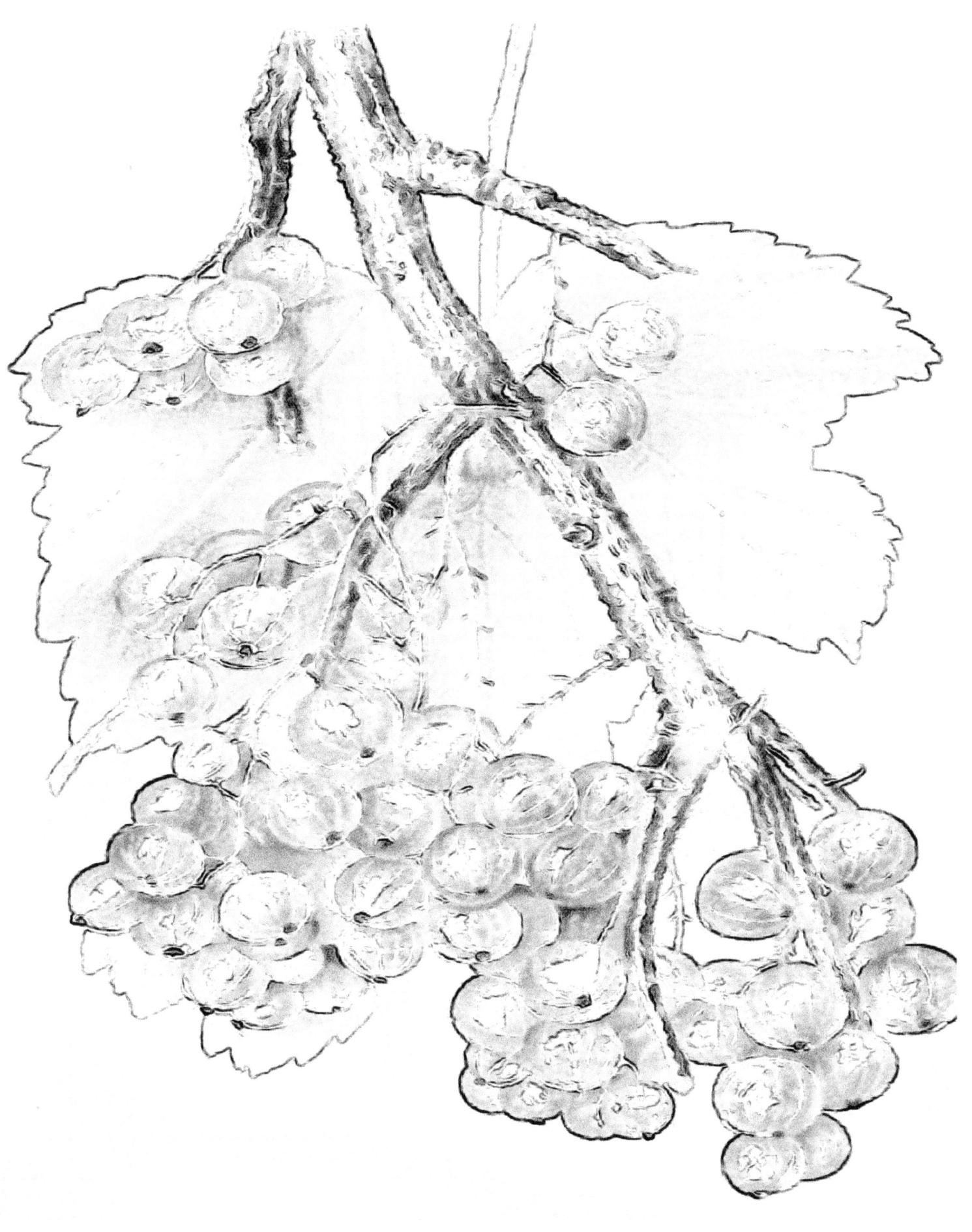

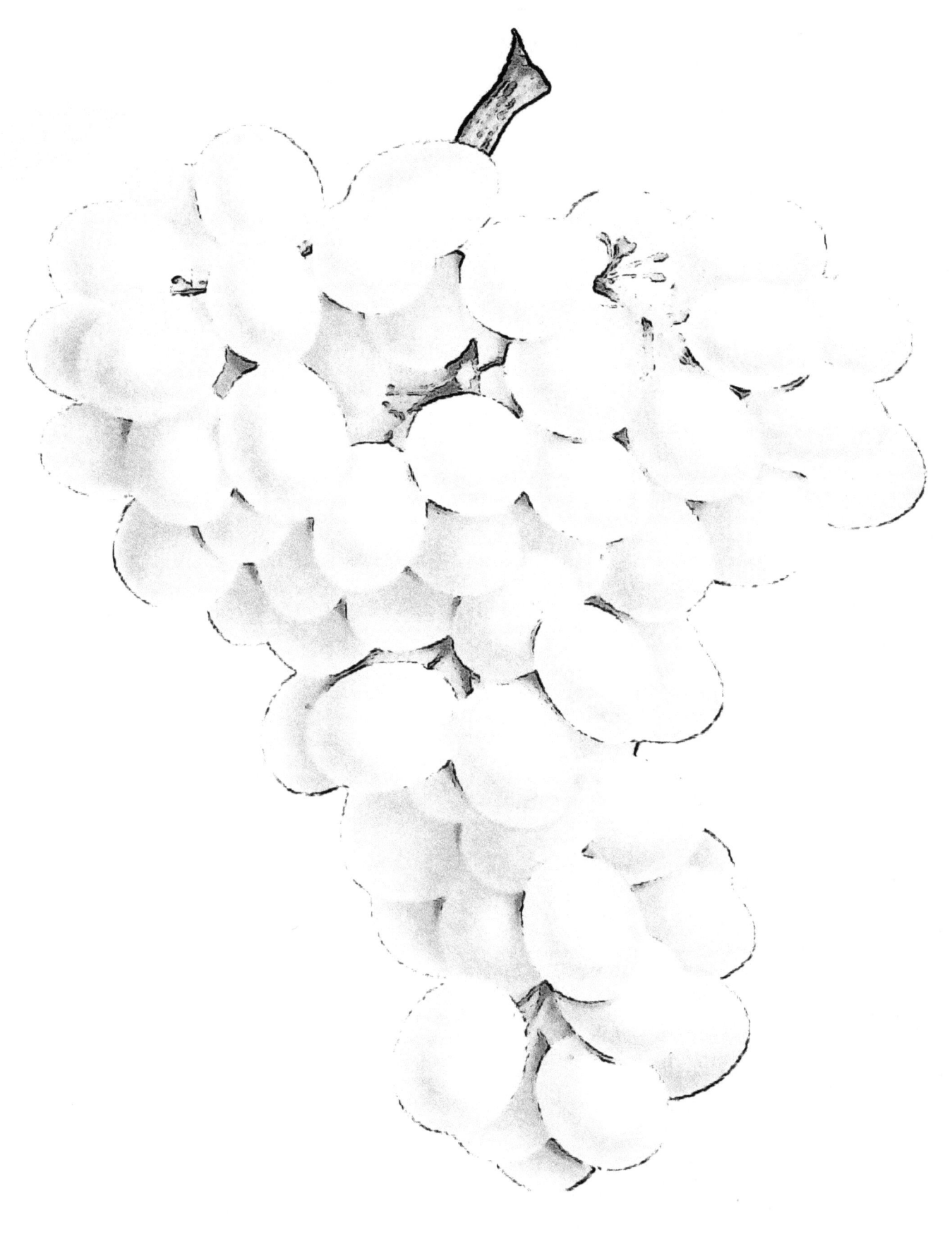

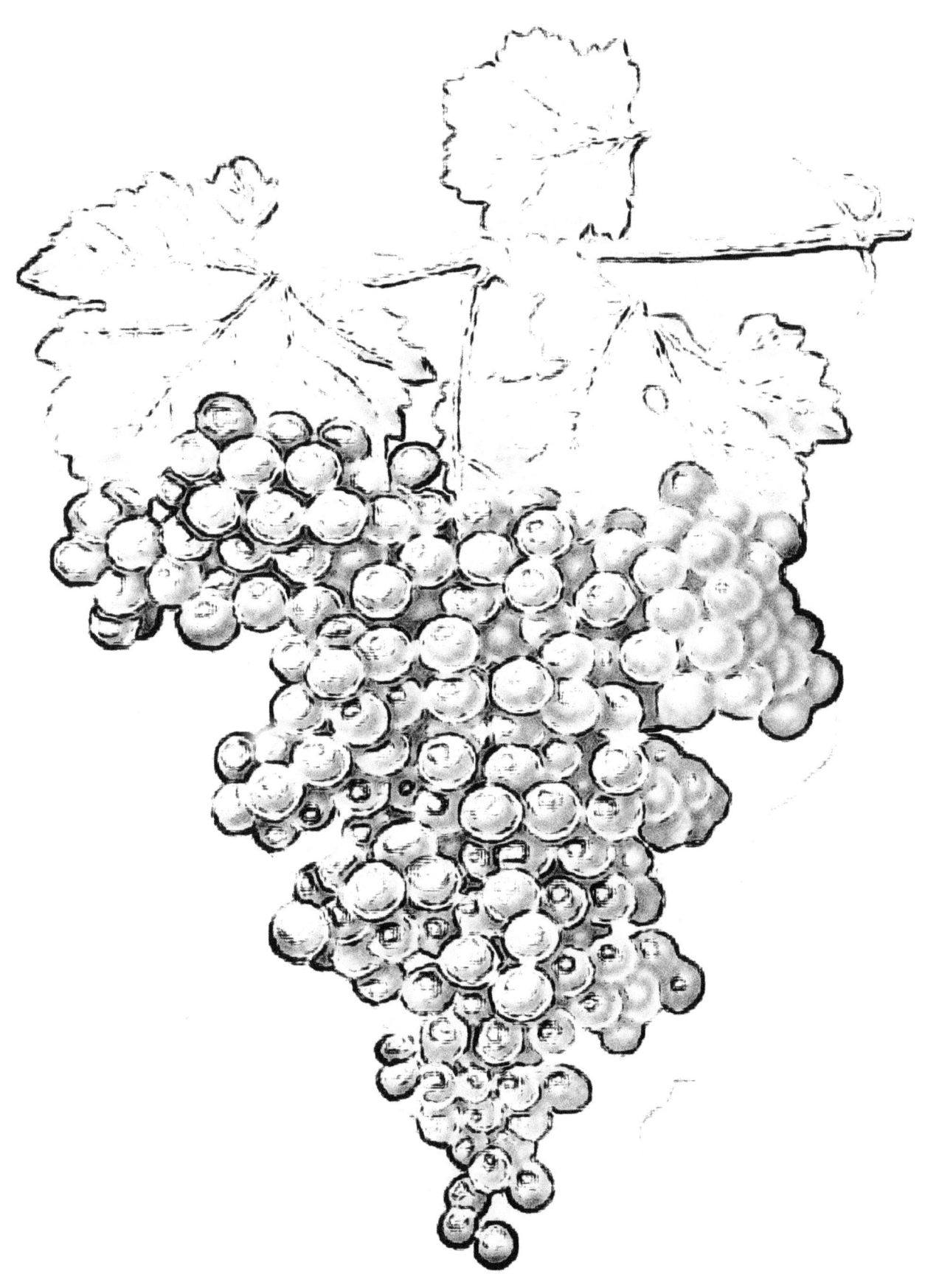

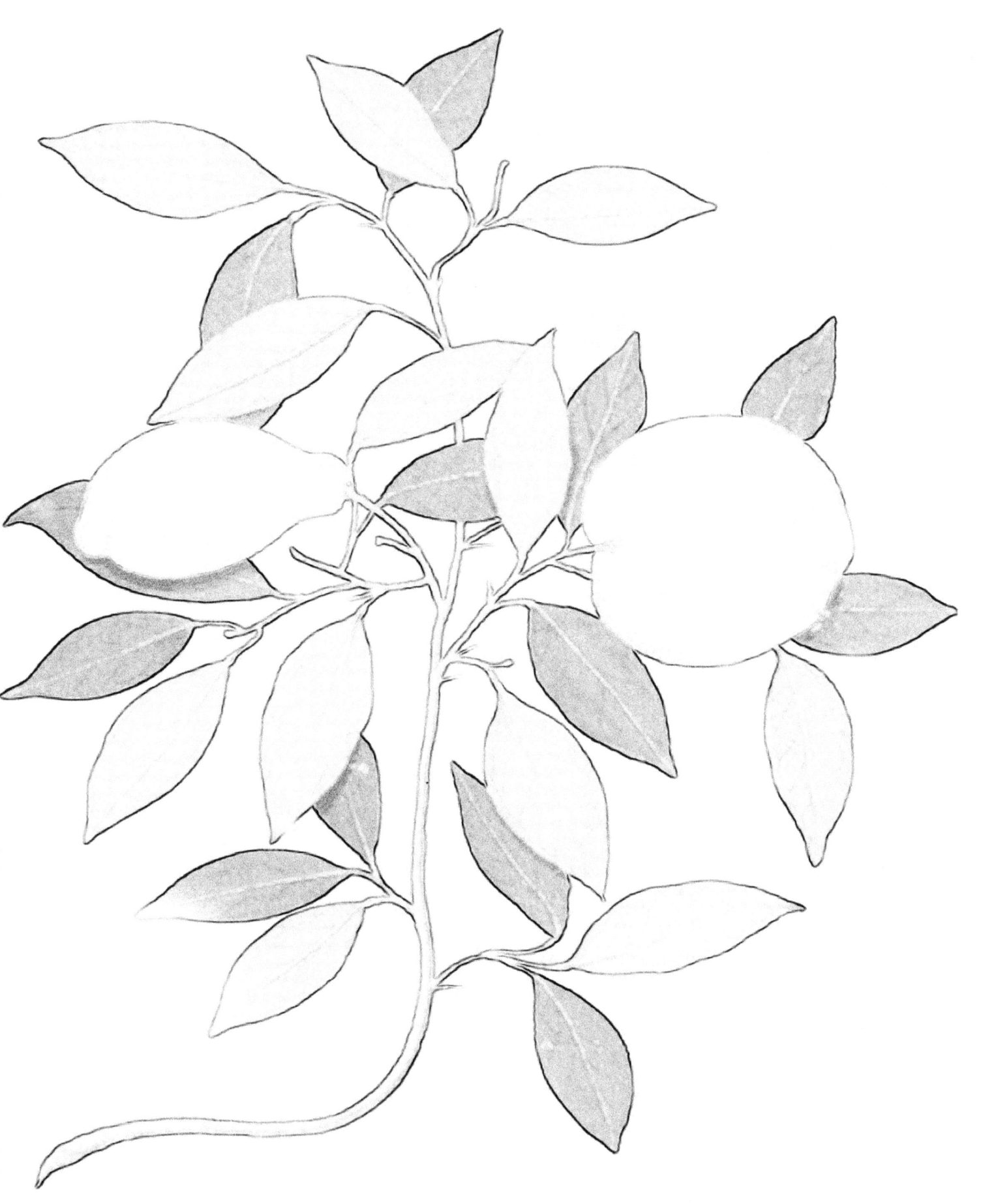

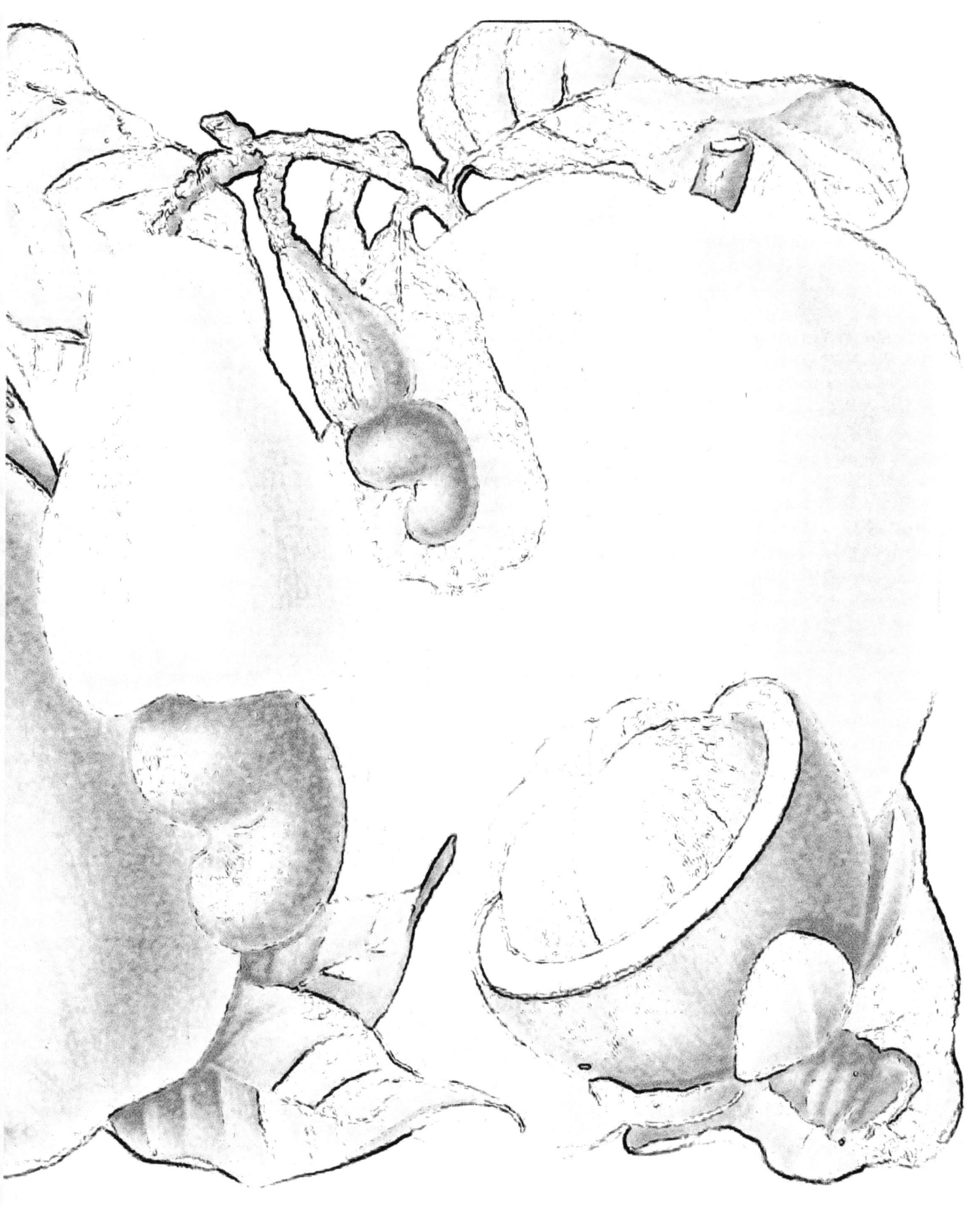

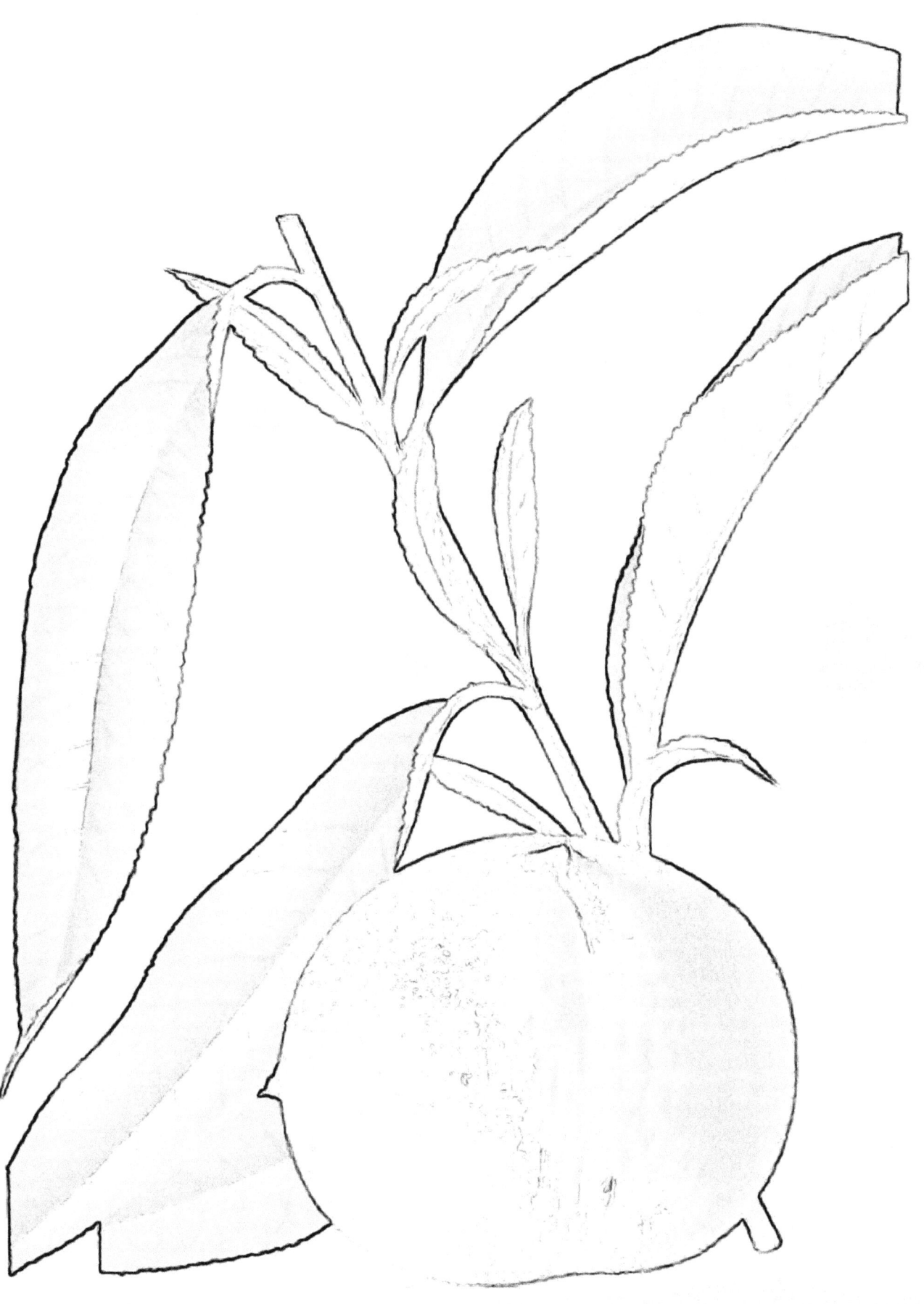

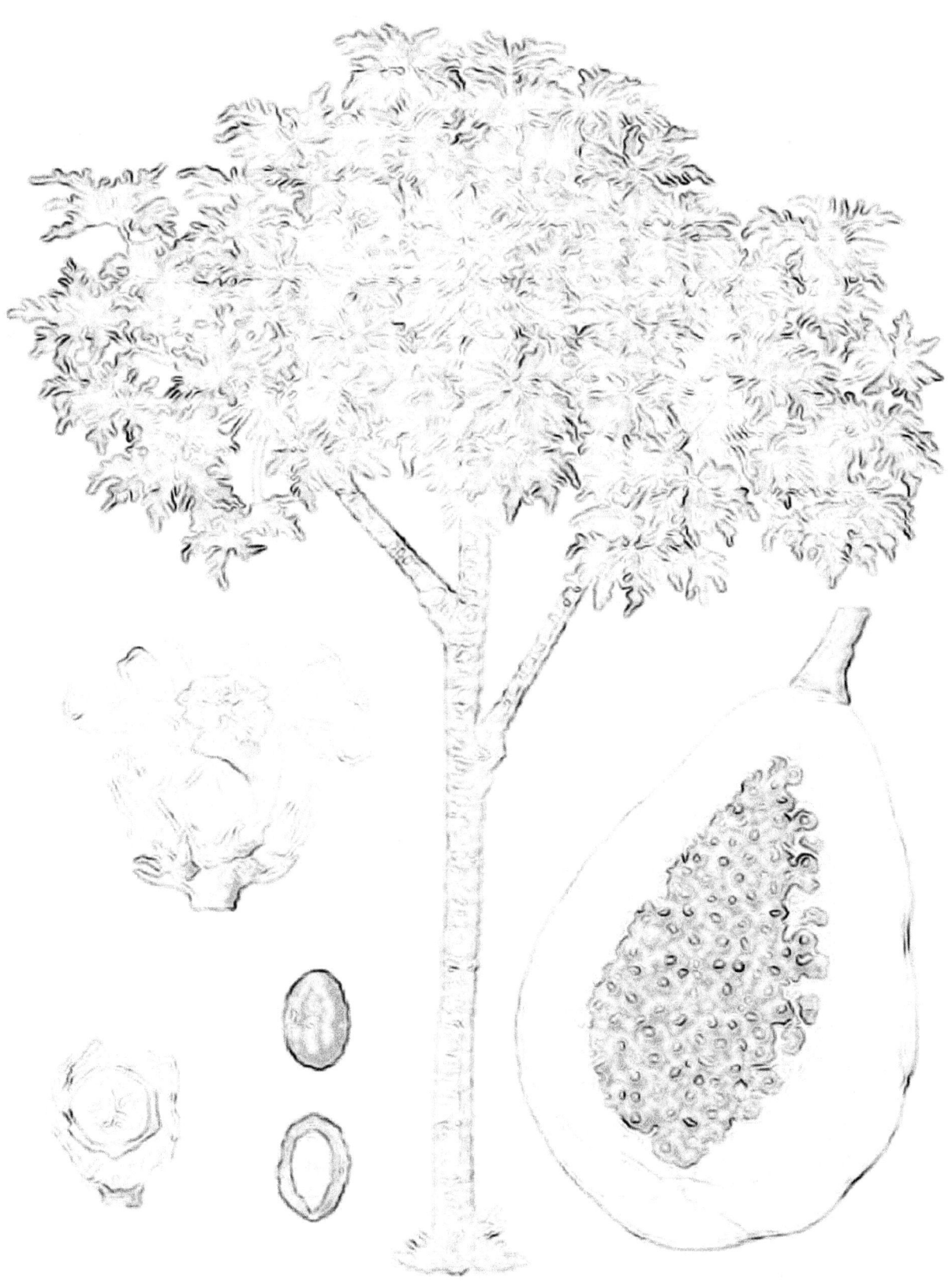

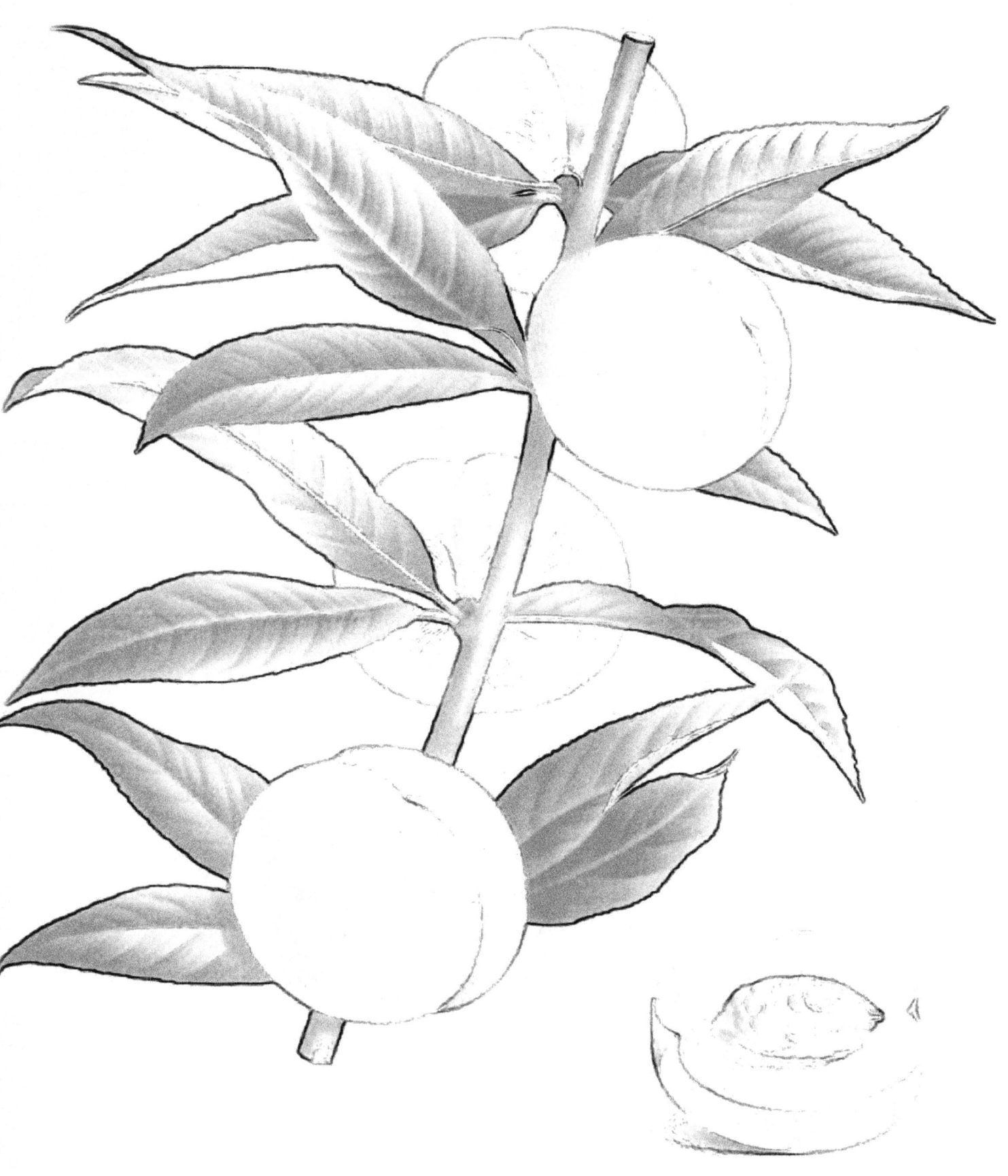

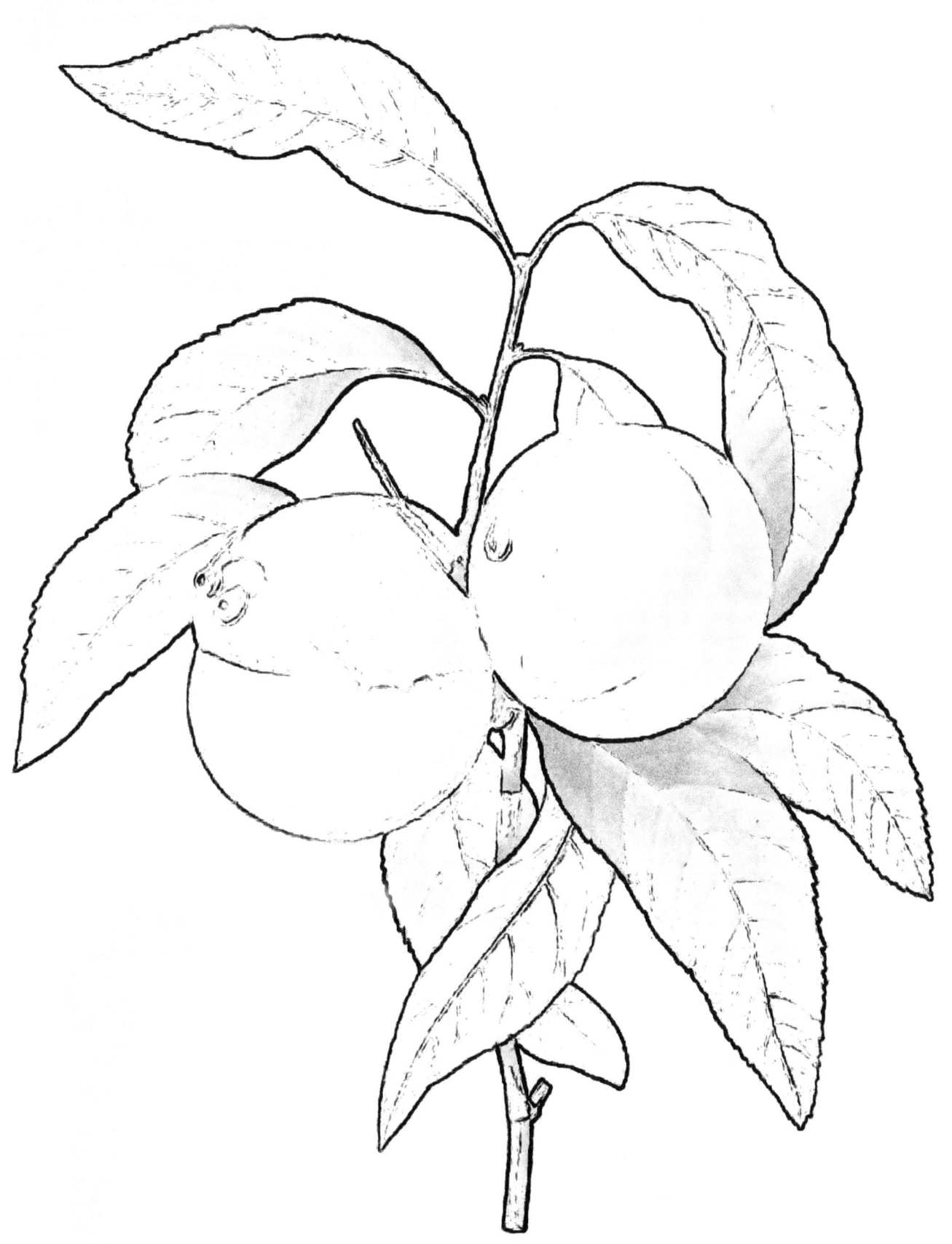

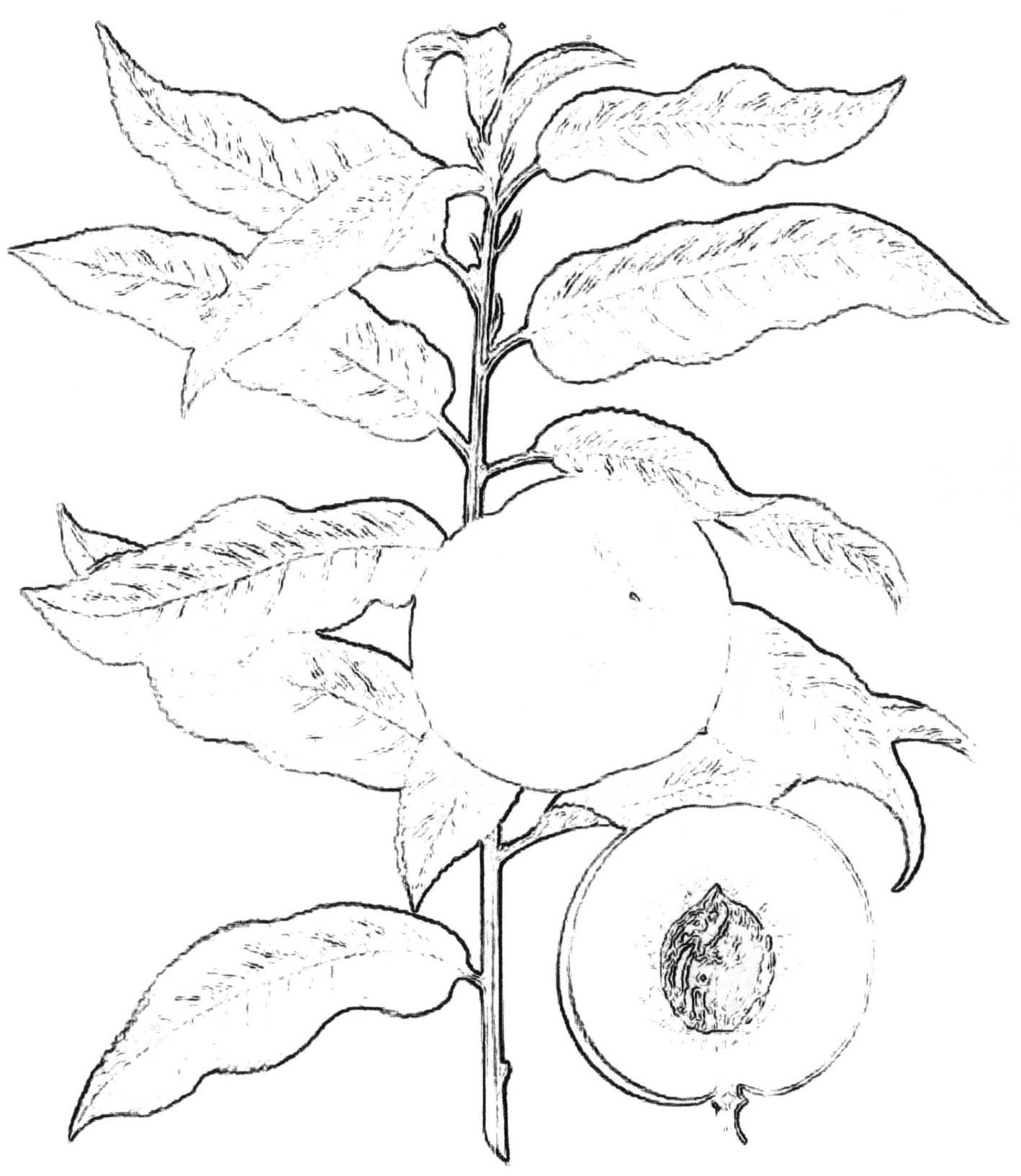

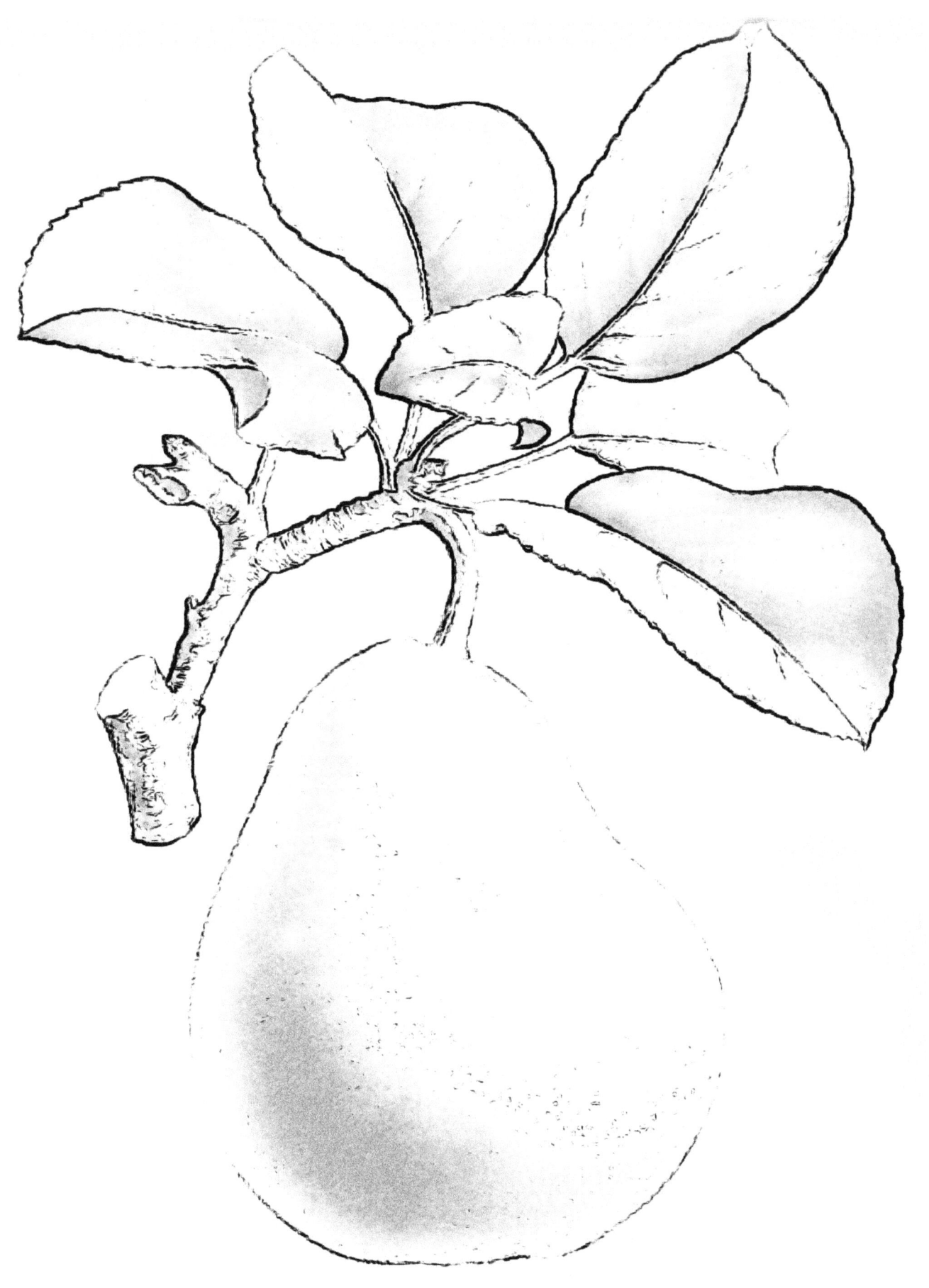

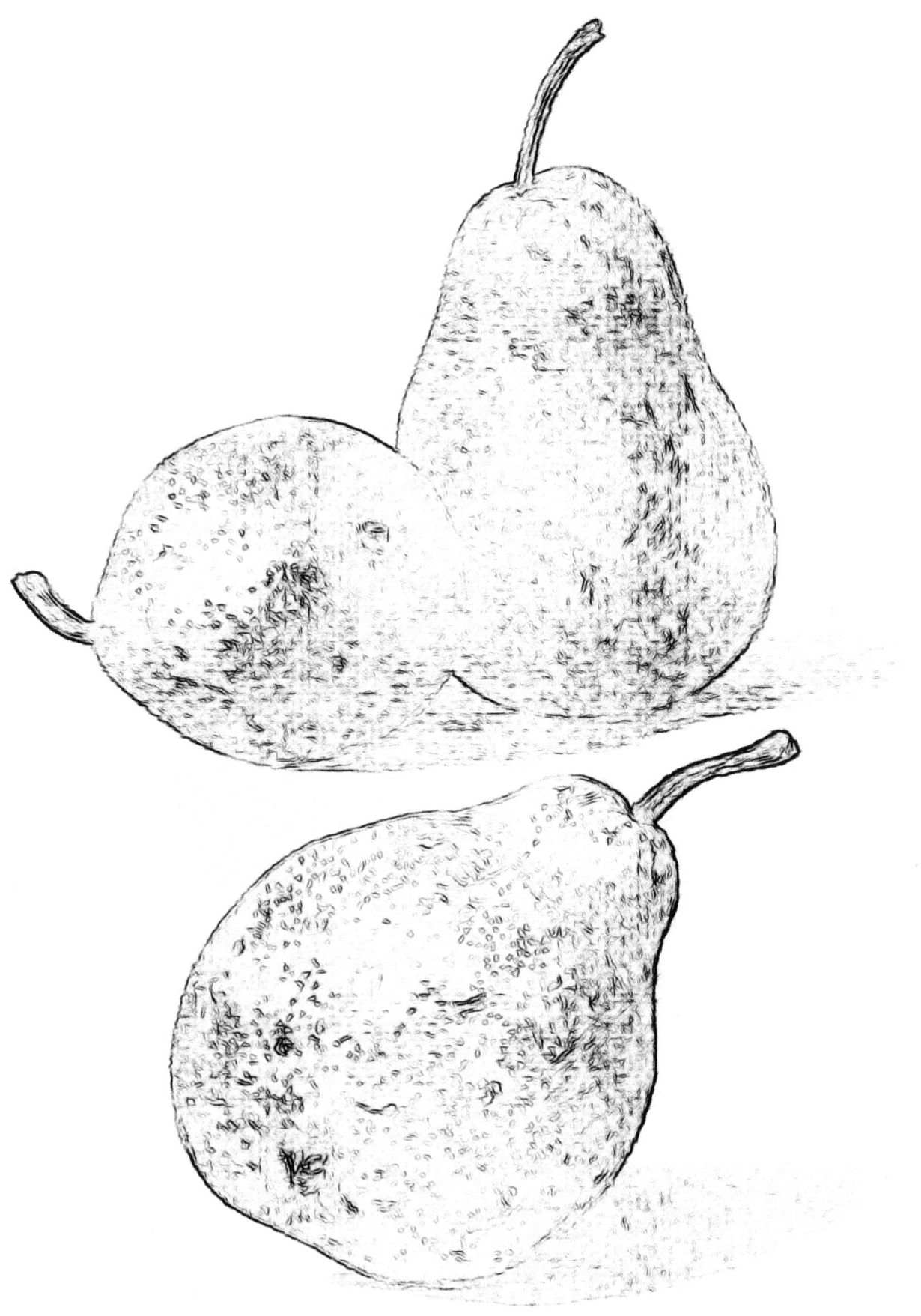

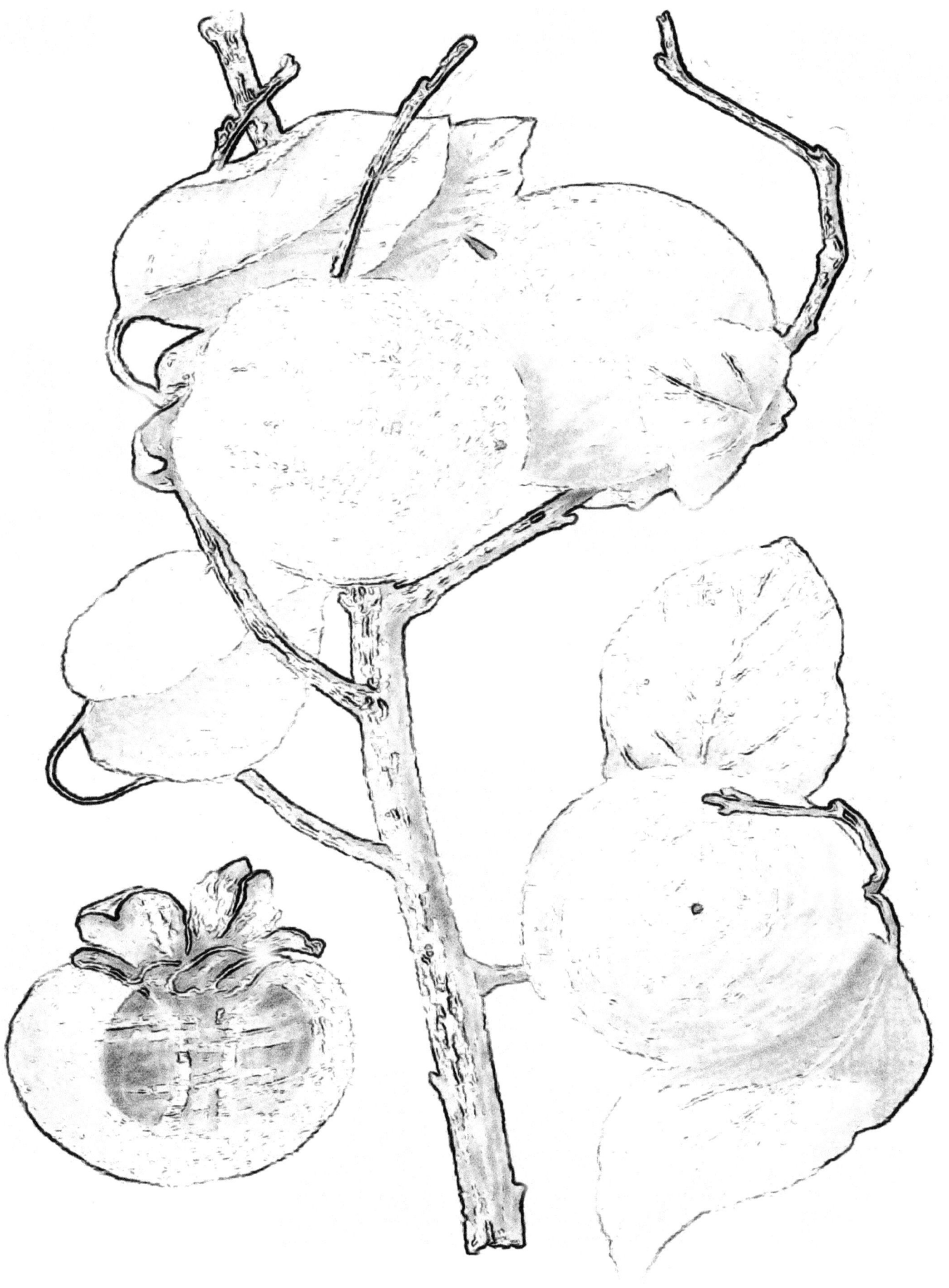

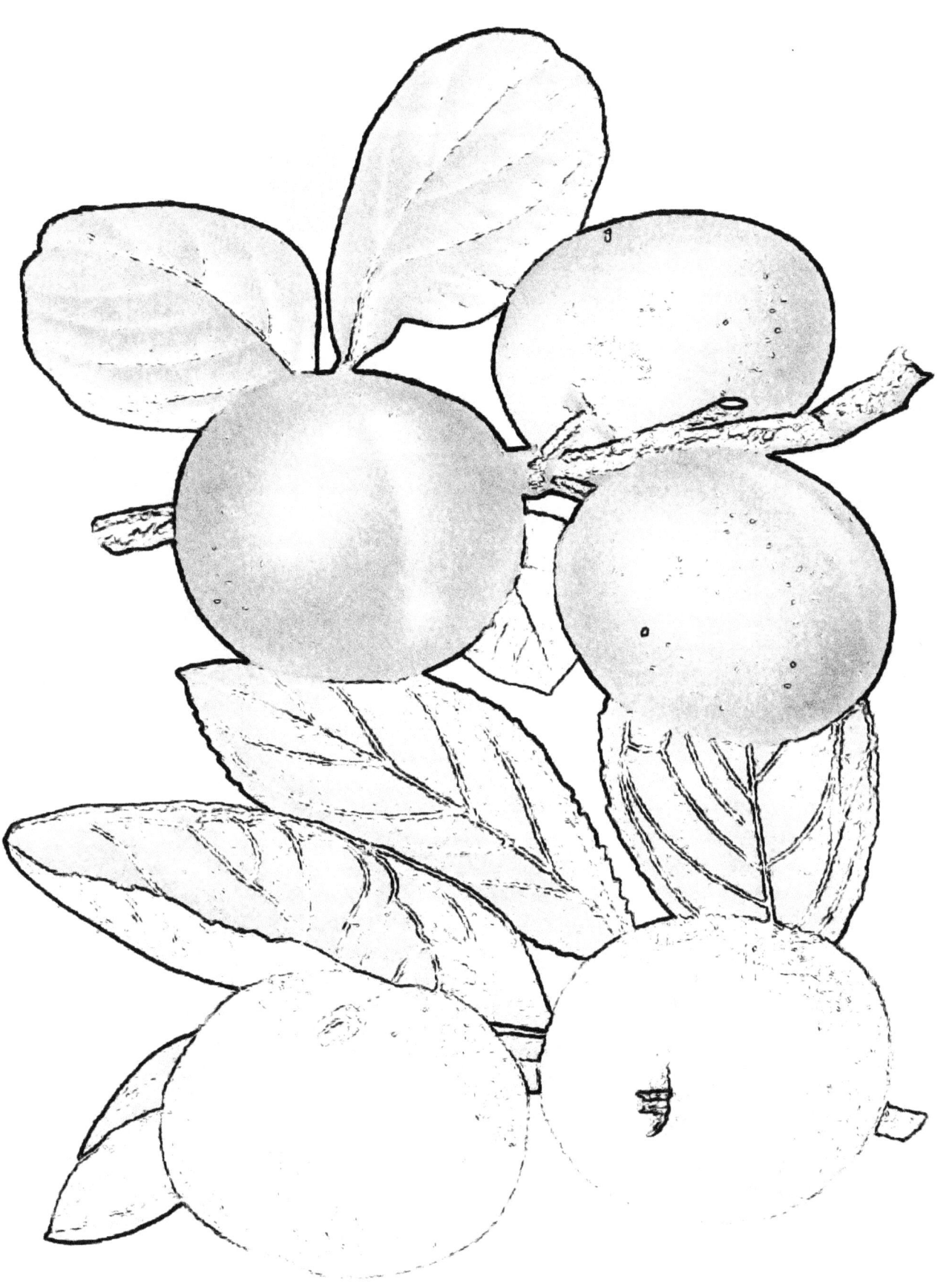

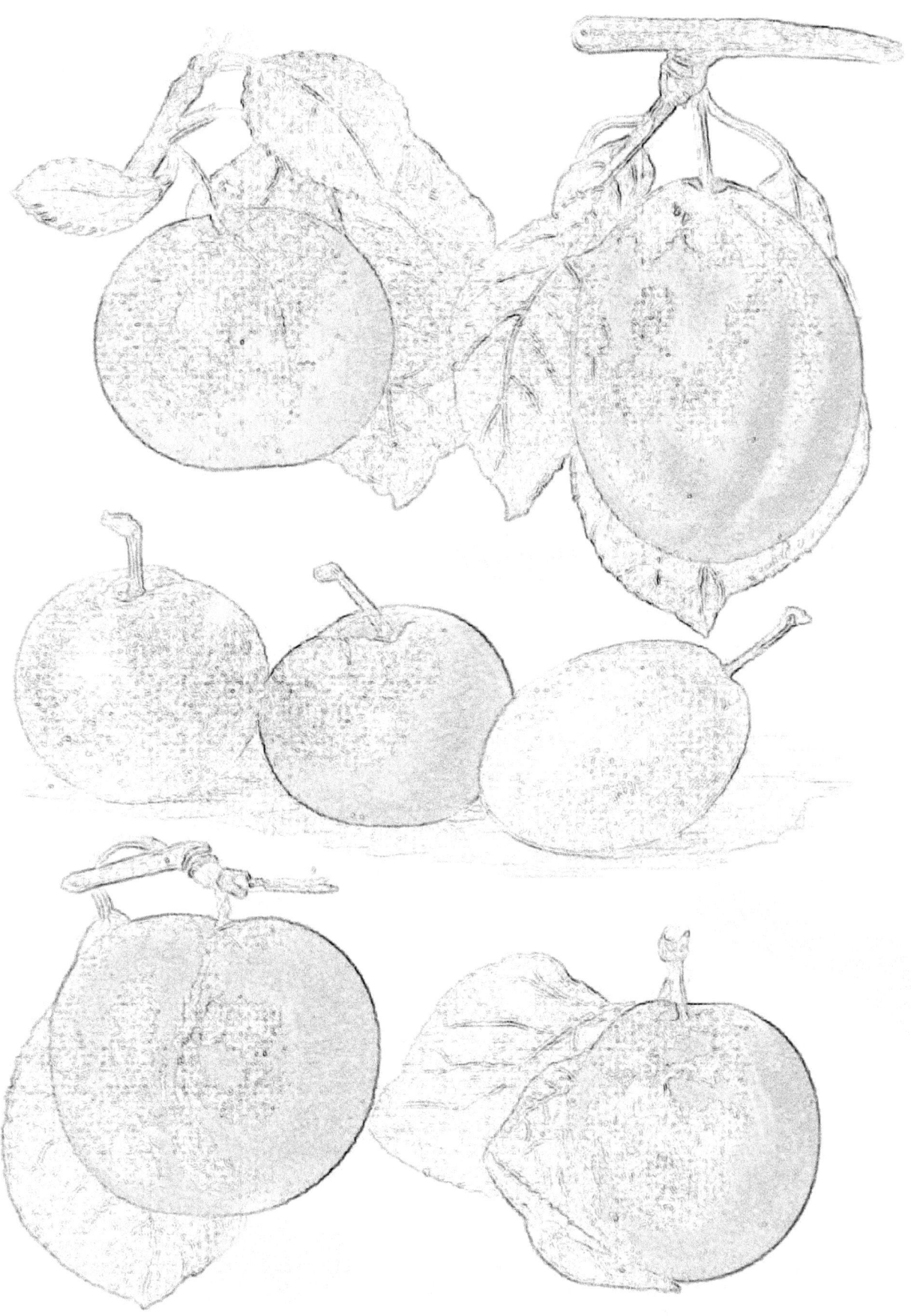

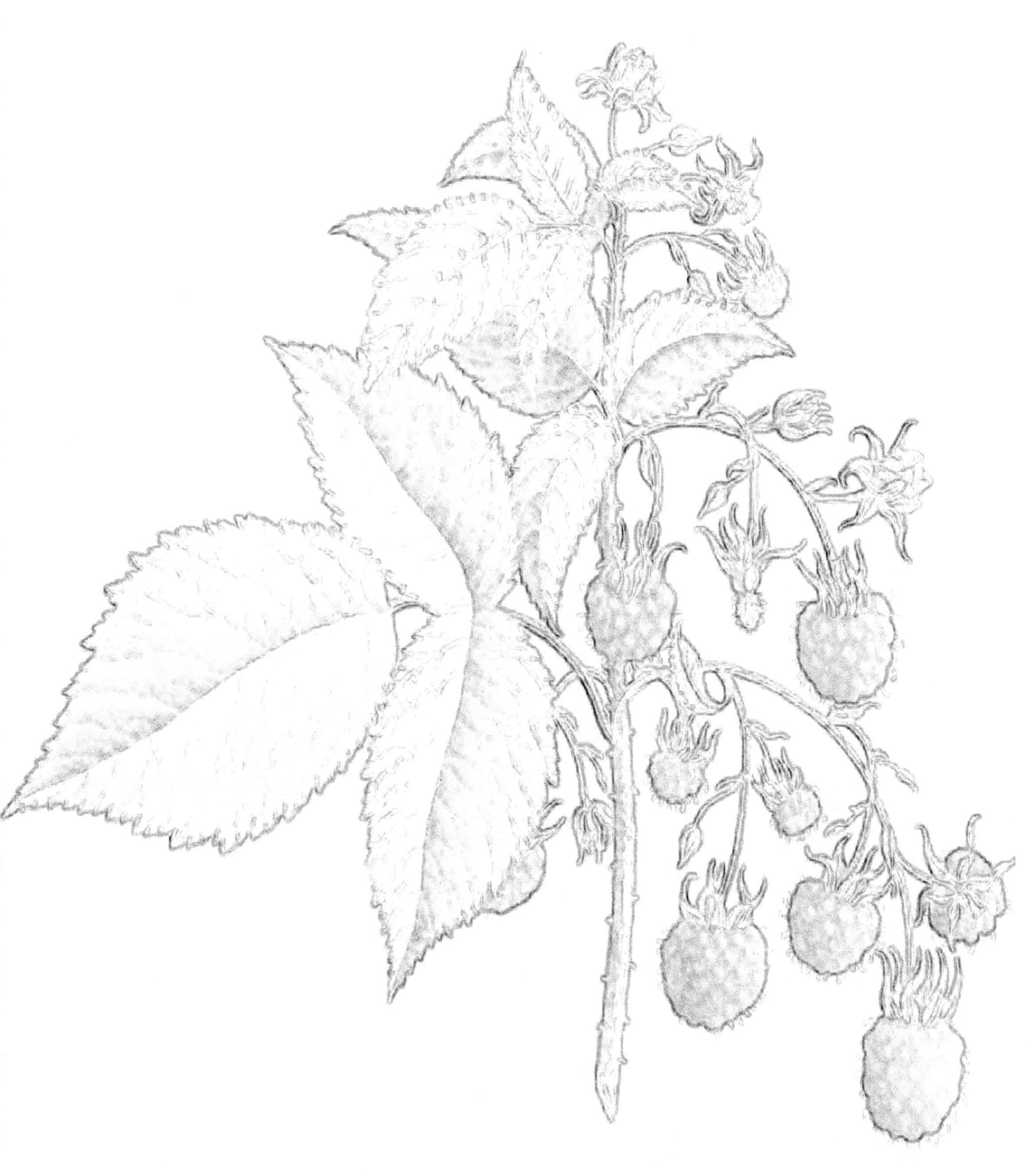

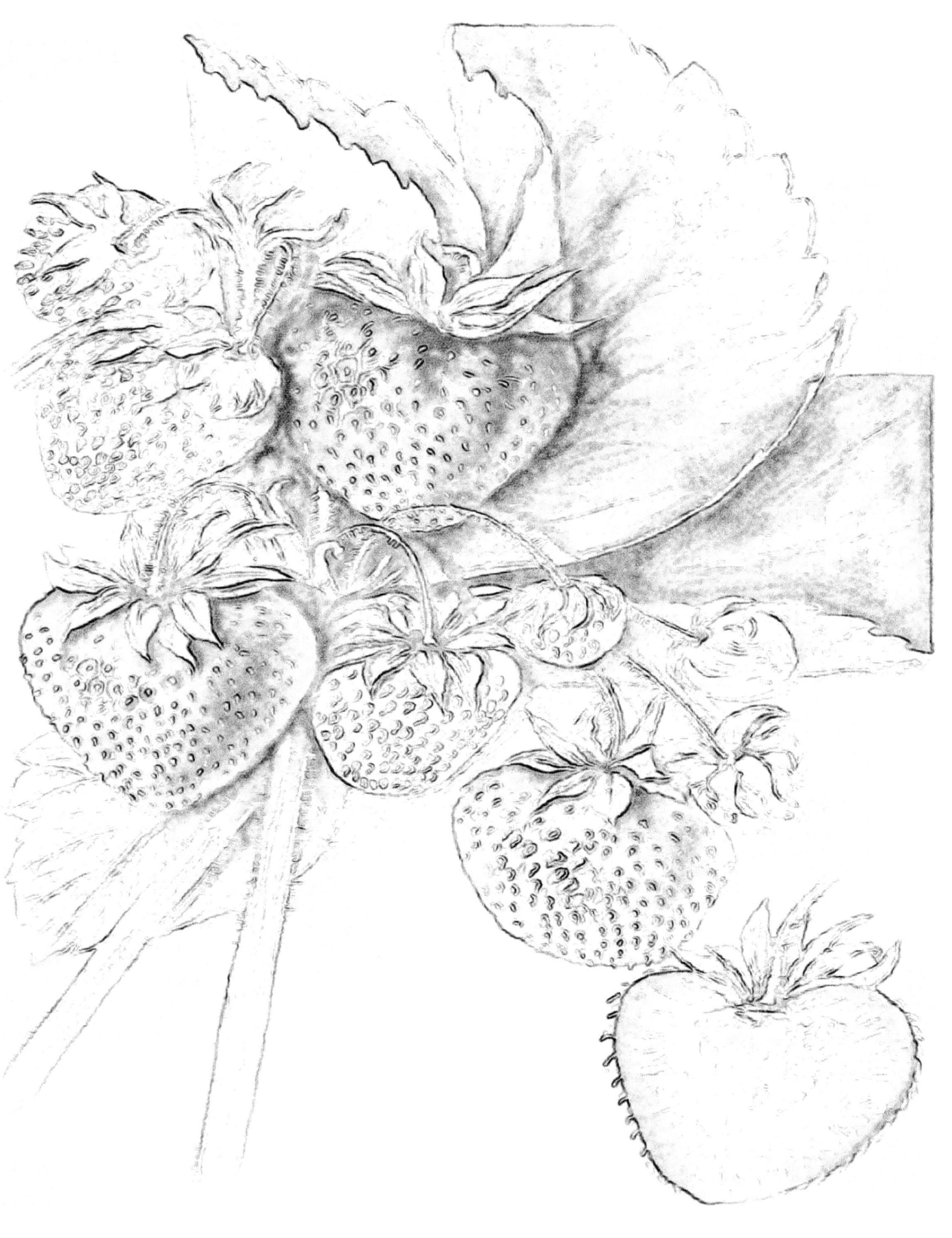

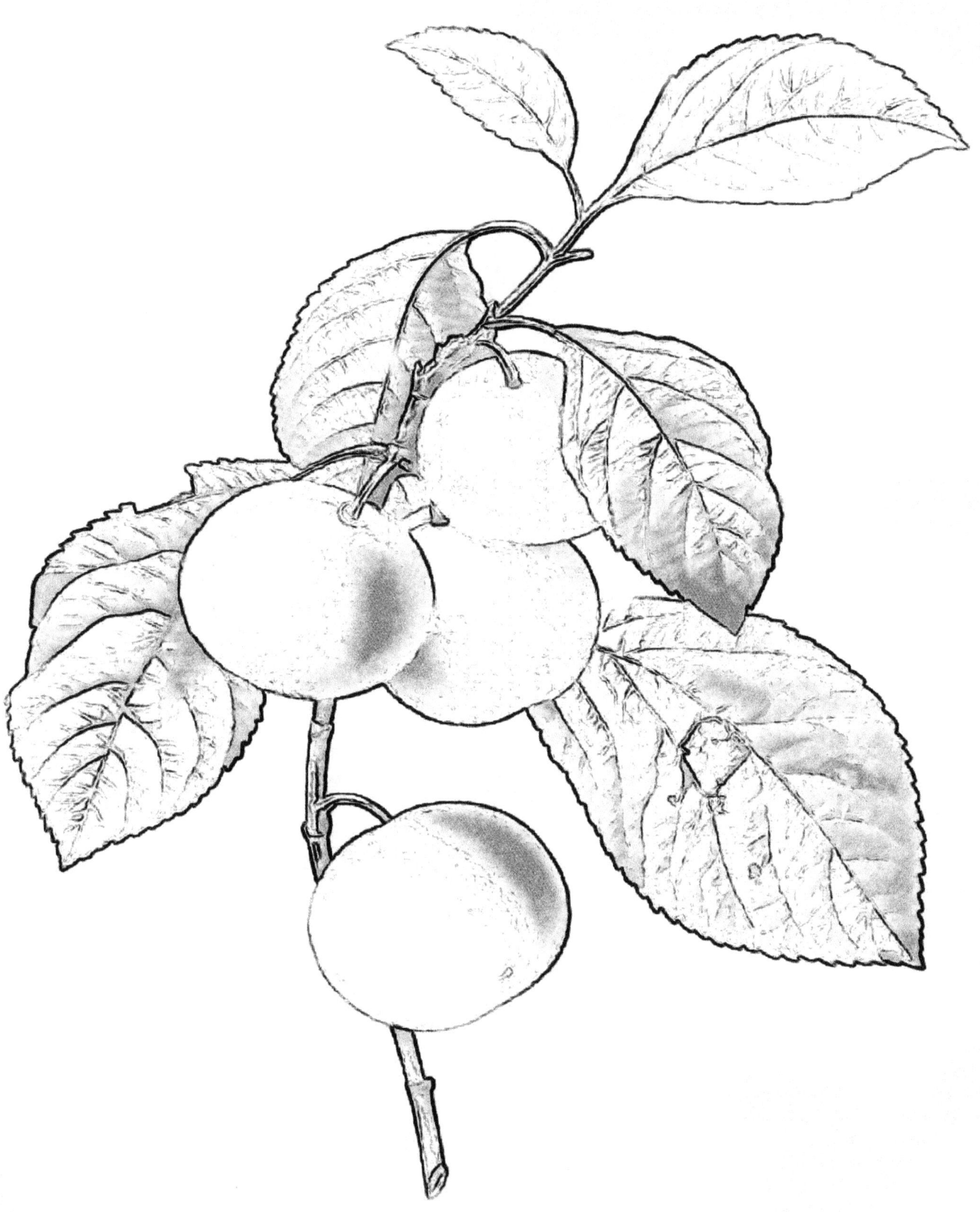

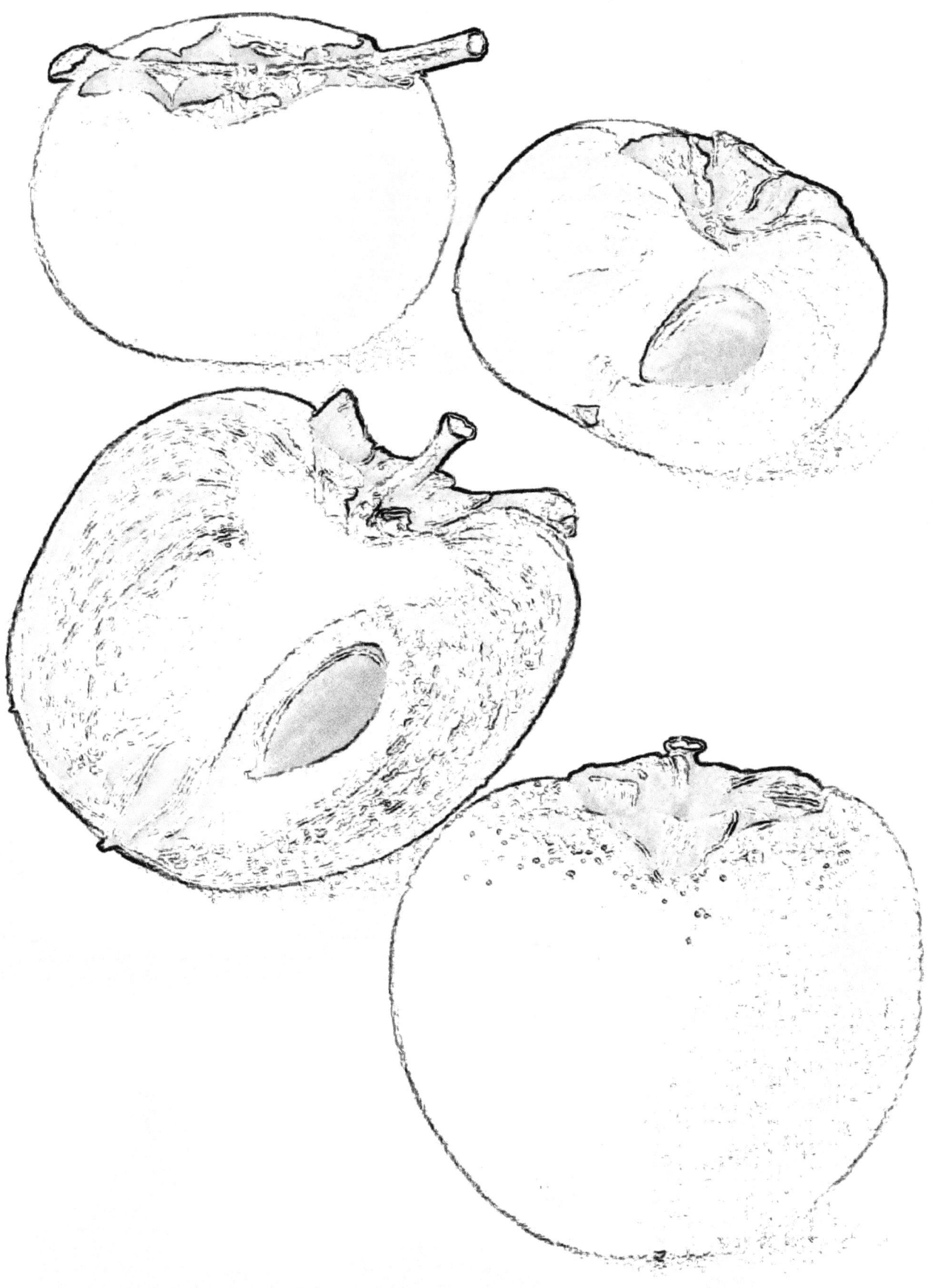

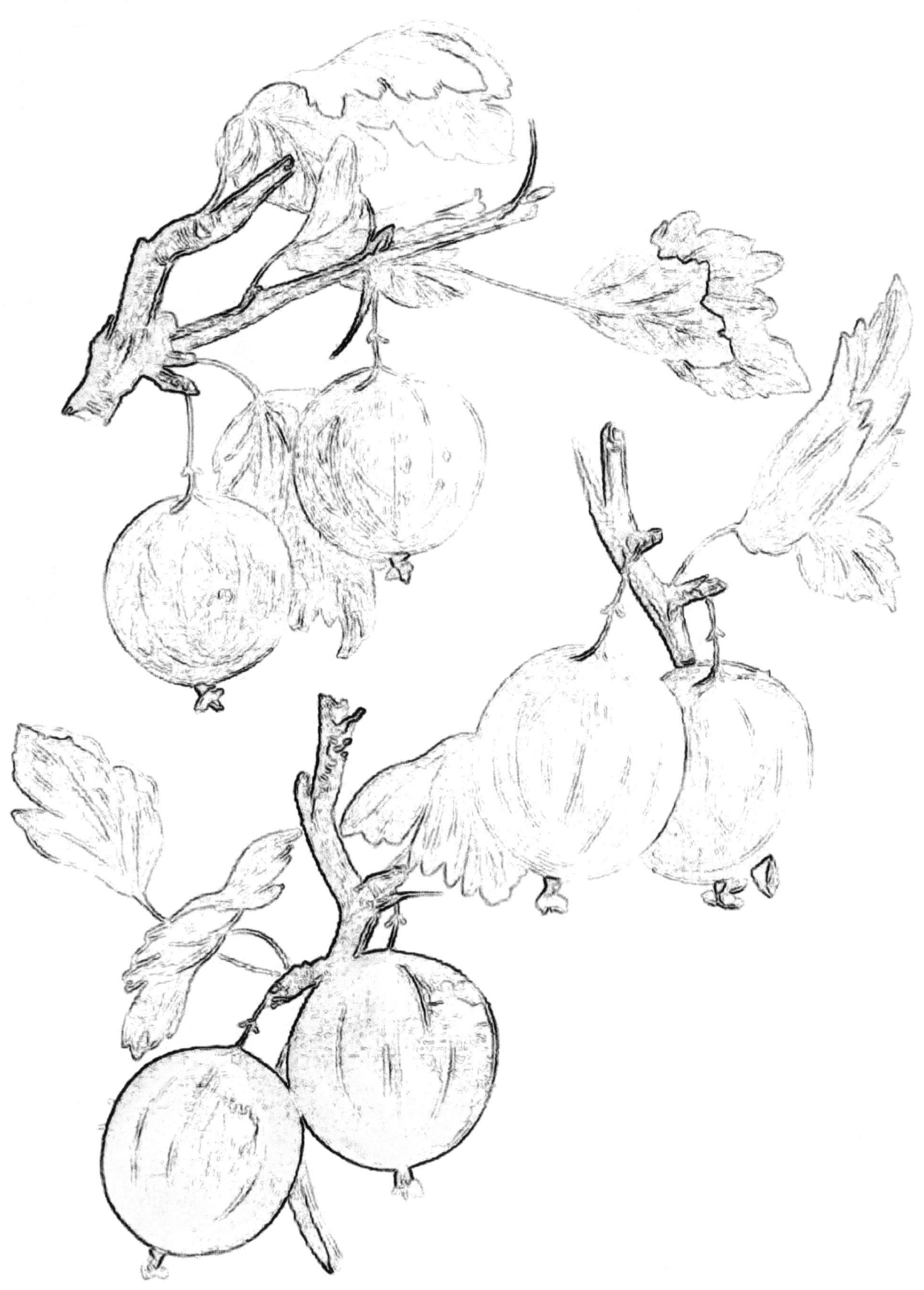

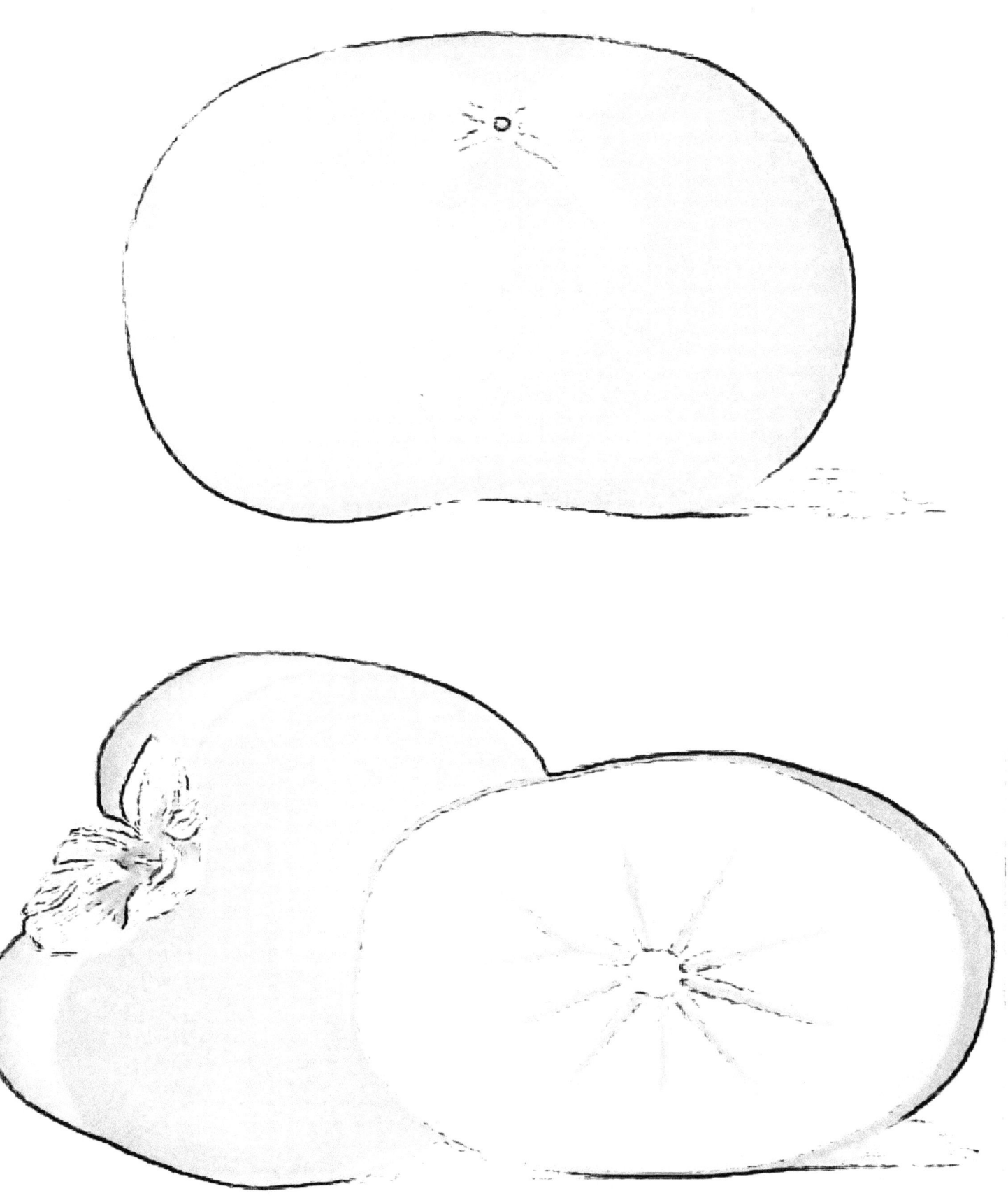

www.ingramcontent.com/pod-product-compliance
Lightning Source LLC
Chambersburg PA
CBHW080555190526
45169CB00007B/2791